# nuevo vino

# nuevo vino

poems, pandemic, pulpitries

**debgrant**

Nuevo Vino
by Deb Grant

Copyright © 2020 by Debra R. Grant
All rights reserved.

ISBN: 978-0-9824226-7-0
jazzwater.com
Houston, Texas

To my readers of
ELOGOS

## TABLE OF CONTENTS

Introduction ..................................................................... 9

One Day Closer to Easter ............................................... 11

The Old Manse ............................................................... 14

Growing Up Place ........................................................... 16

Metaphors ....................................................................... 18

The Company I Keep ..................................................... 20

A Painted Prayer ............................................................. 22

Christmas Tree ................................................................ 24

Not Everyone's A Butterfly ............................................. 26

Someone's birthday ......................................................... 28

50 cents ............................................................................ 30

Thoughts at a Train Crossing ......................................... 32

Party of One .................................................................... 34

A New Name ................................................................... 36

Gestures ........................................................................... 38

Ashes ................................................................................ 40

| | |
|---|---|
| Box | 41 |
| Presence | 43 |
| Skin deep | 45 |
| Full Stop | 48 |
| Hidden Figure | 50 |
| Note to My White Self | 52 |
| Calling Out | 53 |
| Motion Sick | 55 |
| Common Sense | 57 |
| Reset | 59 |
| A Few White Guys | 61 |
| Pondering | 64 |
| Mother's Day Child | 65 |
| Memorial Day 2020 | 67 |
| Holding the Door | 69 |
| On the Edge of Tears | 71 |
| An Extra Button | 73 |
| Shekinah | 75 |

The Room Where It Happens ................................................. 77

Maundy Thursday 2020 ......................................................... 79

Music as Second Language ..................................................... 81

Ode to the Ellipsis .................................................................. 83

Questions ................................................................................ 85

The Endlings .......................................................................... 86

Rehab ...................................................................................... 88

Lantana ................................................................................... 90

I Wish ..................................................................................... 91

About the Author ................................................................... 93

## Introduction

The book in your hands is the product of a new growing season. Two years ago, I stopped a 37-year career in parish ministry. I let myself lie fallow for a time and then felt a call to move from pulpit to poetry though my poetry still has flavored notes of pulpitries. Nuevo vino means new wine, a fitting title for this time of new growth, new fruit, new communion. I began a fresh journey of recalling the roots of fear and joy and the presence of the Spirit.

During this same time, we have all been thrust into the chaos of political upheaval, a pandemic, the exposed wound of centuries of gender and racial injustices. We are in a long season of living and of dying, of love and hate, of cowardice and courage, of scattering and gathering, of learning who we are. This collection of poems reflects all those themes of individual growth, death and life, these frightening times and an unshakable belief in love and hope.

ELOGOS is an internet blog I started over 35 years ago. It has evolved over the years. Many faithful readers have followed me through those evolutions. The readers of ELOGOS saw most of these poems first. I was encouraged to put them in a form that you could hold in your hands. It is because of their tender presence and faithful readership that I dedicate this book to them.

In this season when we are hungry for communion with our beloveds and yearning for touch, I hope this little book is a taste of new wine and the touch of hope.

Stay well.
Peace be with you,

debgrant

## One Day Closer to Easter

Did Lazarus still stink after Jesus said,
"No death for you today, Laz"?
Did the women at the tomb
smell anything...unpleasant?
Don't give me that
"Jesus was perfect so he didn't smell" crap.

I went to a house on Saturday.
It was a home before the hurricane flooded it over a
year ago. A home before it fell through the cracks of
paperwork and no one cares about that neighborhood,
those people.

Now the house is a tomb that stinks
of mold and death.
And yet a man lives there.
He is dying there.
Fighting the toxins, and cancer, and poverty there.
A gentleman.
We wore long sleeve shirts, long pants, closed-toe shoes,
gloves, and a mask
to enter the tomb this suffocating hot day.
Under his frail and weary watchful eye,
I packed family treasures.
Bagged some stuff for the trash.
I did that while he was not looking.

I didn't want him clinging to what was already
gone to rust and poison.
We herded roaches from one drawer to the next.
Damaged wall board shredded under sledgehammers
and crow bars until the house was stripped
to the studs and shame.

This house will not know Easter
in 3 days or 3 weeks or 3 months.
We were hurricane recovery volunteers
not holy magicians.
Poof! Christ is Risen. He is Risen Indeed!
First, we had to face the stink and the death.
The rest came later, much later, many people.
Our job for the day was to meet
the stink and death face to face. Including our own.
Our own noxious odor of indifference to the poor.

I went back home and stripped out of the clothes that
clung to the smell. Considered burning them.
Took a shower.
Scrubbed year-old flood sludge from my fingernails.

Then I got dirty again.
This time planting seeds in a garden.
Planting dead seeds in soil made of dead things.
and thought about the gentleman whose
tomb was one day closer to Easter.
A garden one day closer to Easter.

I dealt with the stink of my own humanity
one day closer to Easter.
+

## The Old Manse

At my writing desk last night
my hands on the antique oak
and fingering lacquered grain
as a mother might examine a sleeping child's hair.
I wanted the desk to tell me its stories.
It must have ancestral roots.
Could I send a splinter of it
to a DNA lab somewhere?
Would they send me results?
Or would they simply tell me that I am a dead tree?
In Concord, there is
a house that thrums like blood with history.
Emerson, Thoreau, Hawthorne have lived there.
An easy stroll out back and there is the spot where
they say the first American revolution began.
Hawthorne's desk was against the wall
because there was too much beauty out the
window he said.
Even the window itself is etched with history.
A tiny poem
"The smallest twig leans clear against the sky."
Composed it says
"by my wife and written with her diamond.
Inscribed by my husband at sunset, April 3, 1843. In the
Gold light."
For now, I have a writing desk

with secrets in its scars.
It is turned against the wall because
my window too is distracting me
with its own romance of pine needles and cloud.
I will, God willing, write a little here.
+

## Growing Up Place

I grew up inside
a Currier & Ives painting
of a New England town.
I walked to school,
to church,
to the library,
to the drugstore
that had a lunch counter
and root beer floats on the menu.

The exact moments of sunrises and sunsets
were hidden behind hills
we called mountains.
At least I call them mountains
until some Rocky Mountain friends
laughed at me.

The terrain of New England
tucks the towns underneath
small shoulders of land.
In the fall, those shoulders
reveal a knitted shawl of mosaic colors.
After a time, the shoulders sloughed the
colors to the ground
where children and chipmunks play.
I had a maple tree.

I claimed it as mine.
It grew outside the bedroom window
where I grew.
It splashed vermilion and fire on my wall.
When I stood beneath it,
the tree sent whirlygigs of seeds into
my hands to marvel at – as if to say
see what I made for you today.

Now I am many decades and
state lines removed
from the town and my tree.
I have become a saying.
I have bloomed where I am planted.
I am a child again inside
a new canvas of changing hues.

I have brought the colors with me,
with pockets of imagination
and wonder.
I am still in a growing place
with new terrain and trees,
the gift of ground
to sink new shoots of roots
for the new season of growing up.
+

## Metaphors

Retired from the Sunday pulpit,
my head still sees the world in metaphors.
The little preacher still lurking in the folds of my brain
goes "That could be a sermon illustration!"

Maybe this is not occupational hazard,
but a language of the Spirit for us all.
The Spirit is not limited in her medium.
nor does love limit her messages.
The window is flung open
for conversation.

I have had squirrels at my birdfeeder.
Yes, I know there are
squirrel-thwarting devices available.
I have the luxury of time to ponder the dilemma.
As a result, I confess the feeder is there for me.
I want the birds to come to me.
I like to watch them in the courtyard of my kingdom.

Squirrels are also members of my kingdom.
They eat too much of my seed that I have allotted for the
birds each day for my amusement.
The operative word is MY.
I have chosen to like birds
during my morning coffee and
NOT like squirrels.

Both creatures are created
equally, purposefully, beautifully and yet,
I have determined that
I want the birds close
because their behavior is more civilized.
Less piggish.
I suddenly found myself as my own metaphor of
hubris and power.
I am easily capable of declaring
one species supreme and another less so
on a whim.

Damn.

I am still learning.
Creation is still churning out metaphors
even when I have no pulpit anymore.
There is still much I have to learn
about myself.
Spirit is still willing to teach.
But did it have to be a squirrel?
I guess it did.
+

## The Company I Keep

In the room called living,
there are five chairs.
One faces out the window.
I sip myself awake with coffee there.
The morning sun is both glorious
and impossible on eyes squinting into a
a laptop screen that reflects my disheveled face -
the face I have been told often
is hard to read.
The other chairs are for daily companions.
One is a child full of fear, wanting to belong,
willing to morph into whatever is needed.
One waits for a friend and a glass of wine.
One is a Jacobian wrestler struggling
through the night with problems bigger
than her weight class. She has a nasty limp.
One is holding space, like Mary, like Elizabeth,
like a tomb, like a sea surf drawing the waves back
and leaving the beach empty...for a powerful moment.

The challenge for me and, perhaps for you too,
is NOT to fill the chair that is holding space.
The others in the room called living:
The child,
the wrestler,
the squinter,

the waiting one,
all need the one who comes
who is bigger than the mystery,
the length of the night,
the weakness of our sight.
Love chooses to come
and sit in our worst company
to make space for
toys of joy,
a night of peace,
a living room.
+

## A Painted Prayer

I got a fountain pen
the other day.
It feels old school.
It needs attention to be filled
and kept clean and alive.
It needs to be held
just so
to connect the synapses
firing in my soul
to reach the nib.
It became a new vehicle
for my prayers.

I got out my watercolors
that need to be woken with
a splash. It needs the right brush
with more water at the ready.
I painted the prayer.
Watercolor is good for prayer.
It makes you think you are
in control of the conversation,
but you are not.
The water does what water does.
The paint surprises with
color, intensity, whisper, and movement.
We get to participate

because that is
how the designer crafted
our divine parts.
The pen, the brush, the paint
and oh, the water.
How the water soothes, teaches
and heals us.

We get to participate.
We get to pen and paint,
to stand back and wonder
and rediscover the power
we have within us
to propel into the world
a piece of peace
or lead.
We have the power
to splash blood
or beauty.
+

## Christmas Tree

My Christmas tree was made
from pallet wood
from Hurricane Harvey-ed homes
rebuilding.

The tree was made
with slats of wood
painted by a friend
named Thelma.

She painted while her
husband worked to
fix the lights in a Harvey-ed home.
She painted while a disease was
stealing her memories.

Thelma painted and hummed hymns
so deeply planted that
the roots of her music tree
were still
beyond the grasp of the
memory thief.
She painted the wood with her melodies.
After Christmas the blue slats
that Thelma painted
became art to sell
to help the people still

in Harvey-ed houses to
have a Christmas tree again
in their own home.

My Christmas tree has
a story about
never forgetting how to
love.
+

## Not Everyone's A Butterfly

A monarch butterfly
emerges resplendent
after an appropriate length of time
in a delicate pupa without windows.
The process is hidden from sight
until the pupa becomes translucent
revealing the stained-glass pattern.
Then the shedding of the delicate layer,
the unfurling, the stretching of glorious wings.

I am not a monarch butterfly.

It is a different process for a furry, scruffy moth.
The caterpillar had to slough off its skin several times.
Over and over again.
Convulsing to stretch its long tail
from the confines of decaying skin.
And then it ate the skin.
Oh, goody, it recycles.
Finally, after a series of slough and eat,
a really ugly cocoon is built
of what looks like vomit spittle.
The cocoon doesn't sleep. It convulses.
What emerges is
something only a mother could love.
Wet, squeezed out of shape, exhausted,

but it has no time to waste.
Life is short.

It finally becomes what it was meant to become.
A scruffy looking moth
with bedhead hair
and a complexion of beige and gray.
Not a monarch.
A moth.

The only difference between the moth and me
is that I will bemoan my fate of being moth
not monarch.

Slowly convulsing comes wisdom.
It is no less a miracle
that once I was a caterpillar
made of dying layers of skin that
I had to shed and eat to survive.
Now....I can fly.
Don't know for how long or why or how far.
It wasn't a pretty process.
I am still really scruffy,
but I can fly.
+

## SOMEONE'S BIRTHDAY

Today is someone's birthday.
Perhaps you know someone born today.
Famous or not so much.
Some parents make a child's birthday
a big deal. The cake, the gifts, the paper hats.

The adulting comes
when we notice that no one notices
unless we point it out.
"Today is my birthday" on the lips of a child is
delicious and delightful.
From an adult, the words sound pitiful.
Maybe because the number of candles
waxes over the frosting.
Perhaps it dawns on us that the day marks an event
where we were present, but we cannot remember.

Today is someone's birthday
and I suspect -and I am only guessing-
many of them are grumpy or worse, unloved.
I know someone born today.
I am glad she was born.
She grew up to engineer mechanics,
to fly, to go very fast without killing anyone, to fit
miraculously into another person's life, to rage again
injustice, to love cats and to be kind to me.

She's just one of a bazillion other people whose birthday is today.
Each of them worthwhile.
Each of them a gift.
Each of them their own delicious cake.
We need not count the candles.
Today is someone's birthday.
If it's yours,
I am really glad you're here.
+

## 50 CENTS

I bet my brother 50 cents
that I would never marry.

I was maybe nine years old
at the time.

50 cents was a big deal.
It was the biggest coin.
It had heft.
More than any paper money to me.

I meant it.
The never marrying part.
I didn't hate men
or women
or the idea of marriage.
I just knew it wasn't
for me.
I just knew it.

Decades later
Now
I wonder how and when to collect on the bet.
I haven't seen my brother in years.
He is on his third spouse.
He is a big fan of marriage.

I am a big fan too.
I am a protector of the dream of it.
I know in my soul
what I am missing.
The human opportunity to be my best
and my worst
in the presence of another human who knows it.

There is much more I don't know about marriage.

But a 50-cent piece still has heft.
+

## Thoughts at a Train Crossing

I put my car in park at the
railroad crossing watching train car after another.
Tanker containers, mostly all black
Heading in the direction of the port or refineries.
Empty or full.
Clack, thud
Clack, thud.
I was in no hurry.
One with graffiti rolled by.
The word "Boobs" in bright white and yellow.
I started a one-sided conversation
with the unknown artist.
I edited my opening lines because they all sounded like a grumpy generation
who hates just about everybody.
"Foolish kids"
"Haven't they got something better to do than vandalize private property?"
I went from grumpy to sarcasm.
"Really? Boobs?
in 3-foot font on a chemical tanker?"
"Kid, I wouldn't dream of painting the name of one of your body parts!"
"What an idiot!"
"Get a job"
"Get a life"

"Grow up!"
Clack, thud.
Clack, thud.
I was in no hurry.
I thought about the artist again the next day
In the mammography screening room.
Routine checkup.
Clack, thud
Clack, thud
My body parts created for the nurture of another generation whether or not they were ever used for that purpose.
An object of fascination.
A vulnerable bags of cells
called silly names on by boys
and drunken breath
or painted in day glow on a tanker car.
The technician noted my laugh
as I stripped to the waist.
"Long story, long train"
I decided to change the subject.
"Do you like your job?" +

## Party of One

A familiar door
into a familiar room
vibrating with the afterburn
of a time machine.
A living room populated
with a cocktail party in progress.
I did what I always do.
look for the exits, the groupings,
the open spaces, the enemies, the friends.
This party only had them all
and only one.
Me.
Different ages, hair, body fat, clothes,
all with comfortable shoes.
I've liked my feet to be happy all my life.
(Pumps are the antichrist.)
I held my merlot close
as if it could protect me
and began a journey of my decades
by crossing the room.

My high school self – moody and creative.
My college explosion of knowledge.
experiments and mystery of a God of love.
The servant making her way
answering a call, stewarding her responsibilities.

I chatted and listened with a new sense
of tender understanding at their wisdom and
their naivete, their shining moments and
their cold shoulders.

I spotted the person I wanted to linger with.
Under the table behind a white lace tablecloth,
she was hiding
just enough to hear the voices, but
out of sight, out of mind, safe
or at least safe enough.
I put aside the wine glass
crawled into the lace tent,
sat hunched and cross-legged.
I asked one question.
The conversation took all night.
The other partygoers were gone
when it was time for me to stretch my legs.
I asked, "What are you afraid of, little one?"
And she told me.
And we talked about her courage
and our feet and how much we
appreciate just one person
who understands.

+

## A New Name

I have been tripping over names for God
lately, oh, let's face it, all my life.
All the names were handed down
to me by ancient ones
shouted their gender.
Lord
Master
Prince
King
Father.
Comfortable names for
when I missed my father, who died
when I was two weeks shy
of my 14th birthday.
Dad, Daddy, Pop were the
trinity of names for
wisdom, love and laughter.

The overlordish ancient names
for God were not completely bad
But were not whole enough
for me anymore.
I whispered the feminine pronouns
once in a while, but they bumped
into unkind mother memories.
I can still feel the breath

of the man who impaled me with a threat
in the narthex of the church where I worked.
"You will NOT call God mother here
if you want to keep your job."
I didn't want to be unkind
even to the face of cruelty.
I kept my whispers to myself
and clung to memories of
a daddy's tenderness.

I had my Deuteronomic moment.
Standing barefoot on holy ground
before my burning bush of a question.
What is your name?
Exposed and vulnerable I asked.
First, I heard silence
as if the other names had to
lift their bows away from their instruments
to let another take the melody.
Then I heard in voice
just familiar enough to trust
"Call me Tender."
Thank you.
I will.
+

## Gestures

When the world seems
to be spinning
out of control
again,
something there is
about gestures.
Small human gestures
that nourishes,
that feels like
a cup of water.

I know you know
what I mean.
You have yours. I have mine.
The gestures are there to
be seen if we are
thirsty enough
to see them.

I was thirsty that Sunday.
My view from a pew
was the backsides of a man and woman.
They stood apart
with elbow space between them
until the Lord's Prayer.
The woman

reached her arm
around the man
and hung her finger
with exact precision
on his back pocket
like she had done
it a thousand times.
Her posture for prayer.

Gestures.
Look for them.
They are there.
They humanize the air
around us.
+

**ASHES**

"Hold my beer and watch this."

Sitting at a funeral, pondering mortality
is a good use of the time.
Humanity does get rather full of itself.
Some more than others.
Dust you are and to dust you shall return.
Compost is the great equalizer in an unequal world. We become carbon residue.
Dust you are and to dust you shall return.
Those words give me pause and then,
I wash the dust off and I am unchanged.
The smoke rises off my extinguished candle.
Defiantly I said, "Remember
you are light and to light you shall return."
I am light. I didn't make it. It is a gift.
I am dust. I can't change that.
We are dust and light.
This isn't a competition. This is who we are.
Life is better when we remember that
while someone holds our beer.

+

## Box

A Twilight Zone episode
set in a diner at night.
A cast of motley characters.
The plot centered on a peculiar salesman
with the power to see the immediate future
in each customer's life.
They didn't think they needed anything
he had in the box, but he convinced them
they needed some small thing.
A coin, a shoelace.
Within minutes, the person with the coin needed
to make a call on a payphone.
The person with shoelace just broke one.
One man looked beyond the box to the power the
salesman had and wanted that power for himself.

I was given an awareness of God
before I knew I needed God.
God was a small item rattling around in wooden box
where I kept old pennies and petrified wood.
Useless and yet, I didn't want to throw them away.

Then came death, change, fear, longing.
I rattled the box. I pushed aside the pennies
and held God in my hand as if
some traveling salesman had placed

it there saying, "This is what you need today."
It started a conversation.
Like opening a window waiting and listening.
I often put God back in the box.
I say this is not what I need...today.
This is not what I want today.
I want the power to know what I need today
more than I want to trust the one who does.
I don't know the answers.
I admit that now.
For today,
that is pretty close to something
that sounds like wisdom.

+

## Presence

Presence was described to me once in this way.

To be present to an object,
let's say a chair,
requires little of me.
Regard its location just enough
so I don't miss it entirely as I sit.
A chair asks nothing, feels nothing.
It does its duty. I trust it to remain a chair
for the duration of my visit.

To be present to a work of art,
let's say, van Gogh's Starry Night,
requires no more than a chair.
It is an object of paint and canvas.
However, if we want to be present to it,
to what the artist offers, it requires more of us.
Time, a sense of wonder, questions & thought, isolation of brushstrokes,
the choice of colors, the impression, the feeling.
Then it makes its mark upon us,
more than a chair, more than the pigment spread
on fabric and frame. Beauty touches us.

To be present to a stranger,
let's say, in an elevator,
requires more of us than chair or painting.

We stand together human creatures,
masterpieces of the same artist. We are mystery.
We share the tiny acreage for a short ride.
Never long enough to make acquaintance,
but long enough to be present to the energy
of our vulnerability and curiosity.

To be present to a human love
requires the most and gives the most.
It is exhausting. Frustrating. Electric.
Joyous. Life-draining and giving.
It is also a choice and a freedom.
We can treat one another like a chair.
We can regard one another distantly as a work of art.
We can stand fully, temporarily, and separately.
We can open ourselves to the other and risk
letting go of everything but love.

What if....God so loves.
What if....God is willing to be present
in every way, in any way,
even as the chair beneath us in this moment.
What if....right now, we are in the presence
of life's finest mystery, of life-defining love? +

## Skin deep

I find it ironic that as we,
as I, age my skin is getting thinner.
The irony is that I was born
with the tender epidermal layer.
No diagnosable illness
just born with a metaphor
wrapped around sinews and bones,
flexible enough to keep my entrails in,
my liver from falling out.

Born with the metaphor of thin-skinnedness
like the tender spot on top
of a baby's uncooked cranium at birth.

Thin-skinned is a character flaw.
Weakness in the land of
only-the-strong-survive.
Born vulnerable.
How does one survive?
No single method works
unless I am willing to be a jerk.
That is what happens when
I let the scar tissue from the
wounds thicken my soul's tender skin
to the point of unfeeling.
To deal with the disorder from the inside is to hide

behind a thicker organ like a spleen or a heart.
Cling to ribs under the cover of lungs.
But in the end, the pain, even
the little ones of thoughtlessness stab and plant
malignant cells of paranoia.
Who can be trusted with this
skin laced with nerve endings
that deliver the telegram of a pain to wherever
I am hiding?

How then shall I live?
Name my flaw. I am thin-skinned.
Live with it.
Don't hide. Don't lump into numbness.
Find a way to live with it.

How then shall I love?
This world does not need more problems.
My friends do not need more pain.
Those suffering injustices do not need my
self-serving introspection.

To love is to live inside each other's pain
without drawing attention to one's own
or denying it or hiding it or cutting one's self
off from life-giving love.
Find other thin-skinned ones.
Hi, my name is deb
I have been thin-skinned

from birth.
I am still alive.
I am occasionally a jerk.
I am very good at hiding.
I am capable of saying
"Ouch" out loud.
I am capable of turning my thin skin
into a protective bandage over another's wound.
Perhaps thin-skinned people
like me
just need to discover the pain is not
as great as the fear.
Perhaps it isn't so much
the thinnest of our skin
but the thickness
of our fear
that keeps us from
loving each other
from the inside out.

We can live with pain.
+

**FULL STOP**

In the midst of the full stop
that the trajectory of our lives
has experienced
in these days gone coronavirus,
do I have any experience or memory
I can draw on?
Body memory or diary or soul-seared trauma?
Any memory of anything
that feels like this full stop?
Snow days are for children, like Christmas,
free and fun and plowable.
I have the stops of jobs ending,
even now a whole career.
The suspension of routine office days,
annual festivals for strawberries or bull runs
no one would dare to cancel.

These days of plague feel more like
that time I was riding a friend's horse
alone through a pasture.
A gentle walk urged into an easy lope,
urged into a gallop.
The ecstasy of wind created,
a powerful creature, warm
and thrumming percussion section
of human, horse, and earth.

And then the horse went stiff-legged to
a full stop.

I don't know why.
He just stopped. I did not.
I experienced the trite but true metaphor
of "head over heels."
It was an Olympic tumbling moment,
a movement of speed and form, blur of sky and earth.
And then I stuck the landing
or it stuck me.
Not a breath left in my lungs even to make a noise.
Shock, then pain,
then feeling the leather reins
still wrapped in my fingers.
Then seeing the rock
my back missed when I landed.
The rock that could have cracked me dead or lame.

Today it isn't a story of being grateful to be alive
or even getting back on the horse that threw me
which I did perhaps because I love a metaphor.

Today it is a muscle memory of
how difficult it is to stop
when it wasn't our choice to stop. +

## Hidden Figure

Katherine Johnson.
I see you.
Now.
I didn't see you when
I watched the space program
on a fuzzy black and white television.
I was my father's remote control
before there was such a thing.
I was the thing sent to change the channel
or whack the console to
jar it into clarity
or wiggle rabbit ears
to make it work.

We worked hard to see
the rocket launches and
the astronaut interviews.
We didn't see all there was to see.
We didn't see you, Katherine
and your coworkers
in office spaces at NASA
calculating figures
so that the white men could
shoot a rocket in the air
and know where it landed.
Now decades and geography

away from where I watched
mission control and heard
the word trajectory,
I live across the street
from NASA.
It is pretty cool.
I drive by recalling my viewing through
a black and white tv, that that I am learning
showed more white than black.
It didn't show Katherine and her slide rule
doing her job.
"They needed information," Katherine said,
"and I gave it to them."

Katherine Johnson died today.
I live across the street from where she used to work
just doing her job in a world
that saw more white than black.
I see you, Katherine, now when I drive by.
I say to myself, that is
where Katherine Johnson worked.
So far away and I see you now.
+

## Note to My White Self

Listen until you
See the blood that's not your own,
Hear the fear like you have never known,
Touched rage that is 400 years old
and still burning.
Don't wallow in guilt. Start learning.
Do justice for at least 400 years
until the bleeding stops.
Have a nice day.
+

## Calling Out

The tectonic plates have shifted.
I have felt it. So have you.
It is not a time to be pewed under glass.
It is not a time for our privileged
sanctuaries of rituals.

Hear me out.
I like rituals.
Take communion for example.
Bread and wine
by hands and into hands
given and poured.
Simple, exquisite, holy.

We make it more complicated.
Perhaps you know what I mean.
The who, and why, and what
and when of the altar dance.

The ritual is lovely.
Some of it is a luxury.
Some are barred. Some bar themselves.
Some don't care.

We are, whether we like it or not,
the remnant for this time.
We are born to be sojourners,

not extenders of temples for
the obesity of our rituals.
It is time for ecclesia -
the calling out of the body,
to travel and attend to travelers,
to share a bit of bread and wine
and cherish the hands
that need and feed, that pulses take.

The time for
ecclesia has come.
You may bring a ritual, if you like,
but one, make it a good one.
Nothing empty that
needs a lengthy explanation.
Let it be of love
and hunger.
Pack only what can
fit in a backpack.
It is frightening, I know.
Let's find a way to walk together.
+

## Motion Sick

I traveled for weeks on a freighter
with a Filipino crew
who kindly offered what they knew
to be true about seasickness.
Through the bits of shared language,
they said, "Eat."
Keep your stomach full.
Counter-intuitive if you are retching
Not spicy food, mind you, or greasy sauce.
Basic sustenance.
Bread or rice or fish.
Solid, gentle. Warm and good.
Don't seek solid ground yourself.
You will not find it
Even on a 900-foot container ship.
Even its massiveness steel
heaves with a wave.
It pitches and rolls
and makes its way slowly.
Remember where you are.
You are not on solid ground.
Shutting your eyes will make it worse.
YOU are not solid ground.
This crew is not solid ground.
You are with them in the tempest and the swell.
Right now,

this pitching planet is where we are.
We are all more than a little motion sick.
We are retching.
We are grabbing for handholds,
but they are not still.
We want the motion to stop.
We will die to make it stop.
"Eat."
says the voice of pure kindness.
Remember where you are.
We are on a moving ship.
Our solid ground, our common ground
is that we are constantly in motion.
The truth will set us free.
Shutting our eyes will make it worse.
When we fight and retch a little less,
we will learn how to
crew this ship
together.
+

## Common Sense

This has been a season
of an assault
on our senses.

The virus if it doesn't kill you
steals your sense of taste
and smell.

The distancing is necessary
but stifles our sense of
touch.

The mask is necessary
but stifles our ability
to see a smile or
a sneer or hear
well.

Some choose freedom
of their senses over
common sense and
everyone loses.

Patience is not our
strength and yet,
if we are patient
our senses grow

to accommodate our
circumstance.

It is the essence of
our humanity
to taste the gifts of clean earth and air,
to smell danger and deliciousness,
to listen more deeply,
to see with the eyes of our hearts
to touch in magical ways.

Please be patient
A while longer
until our senses
catch up with us.

+

## Reset

I have reset buttons
on more devices than I can count.

Those lacking buttons
have plugs that unplug
to wait
one Mississippi
two Mississippi
until enough
Mississippis
equal reset.
Justice.

Power outages
teach us how vulnerable we are
how much we need one another
how fragile life is.

If the prescription was a reset,
how do we push the button
on ourselves?
How do we decide together
to unplug and agree to
move the power around
differently?
How do we know that
when the power comes back

the heart of the people
will find a life-giving rhythm
of a heartbeat?

No one wants to risk it.
The self-inflicted reset.
What if we lose our data?
What if we forget?
Who controls the power?

But what if in the darkness
we hear each other counting
One Mississippi
Two Mississippi
+

## A Few White Guys

I saw a silver lining in the sky
that reminded me of this white guy
I know who moves through
his soul with a hope that
always has to fight its way out,
but it does, and when it does
it spills out over everyone
who has ever had
a beer or a cup of coffee
with him.
It was good way
to start the day.

I thought of another white guy
I know who watches
where the skies explode
into disaster on the land
and then, when the time is right,
he calls together a force armed
with power tools and varnish
and he feeds stray dogs
with kibble he keeps in
his pocket for them.
He wears his love for
family and vets.
He doesn't like to talk about

his faith too much,
he just lives it out loud
rather well.

I thought of another white guy
who is goofy as the day is long,
who struggled to find out where he fit
but when he did, he became a teacher
of literature and journalism
and lit the fire of freedom,
and beauty and truth in
hundreds of lives ever since
a goofy Captain America.

I thought of three white guys
this morning.
I thought of the content
of their character.

I see their whiteness and their
guyness alone with judgement.
If I didn't know their character, I would
wonder whose side they were on.
They would be the first to admit
their whiteness
and their guyness
as a part of who they are,
that it came with privilege,
and is not fair

and they sincerely work to change it.

I thought of a few white guys
this morning
and the content
of their character.
+

## Pondering

I have been pondering.
Pondering is a word that reminds me
always of Mary the Mother
who reacted to life-changing news by pondering.
I have been pondering Michelangelo's Pieta.
Mary with a dead son across her lap.
Mary loving because love doesn't end at death.
Mary suffering because suffering is a part of life
as visceral as love.

I have been pondering Wiesel's Night
that I reread the other day
because it just seemed right.
It just seemed right to lean into the suffering
and embrace life with all
of its love and pain.
It just seemed right
to ponder love and suffering
and, in doing so, enter
more deeply into our
shared humanity.
We are in our isolation
still able to ponder, still able to love in pain,
still able to try to keep one another alive.
+

## MOTHER'S DAY CHILD

I haven't had to buy a card
or make a phone call
on a Mother's Day
for going on a decade and a half.

Now the May day is when I remember
the last gift I ever gave her.
A self-inflicted wound on her behalf.

Mothers and daughters
can be complicated.
Another word for conflicted.
Our womanhood alone makes
it complicated enough.
We pity our diminished power
even as we fight with one another
over the scraps.

We never understood
each other. I gave up resented
her for that and forgave myself
the indignity of not liking her much.

The last gift I gave my mother
was presiding at her funeral.
As my silent siblings and a few
acquaintances watched,

I shoved my bare hand into
her ashen remains and spread
her on the grave of her 2nd husband.
I carried the rest of the ashes in a plastic
tub to her gravesite next to my father.
I said some words scribbled on a yellow note pad.
I spoke of the complicated woman,
the burdens she bore including us children.
I said that no matter the memories or
the scars of the relationship
there was still dignity
in her unique place in our lives.
That dignity will never be taken from her.
It was the first time I walked away from my mother
wounded and still whole.

+

## Memorial Day 2020

This is the day my father
would recite from memory
the poem about the poppies
growing row on row.
A car accident put him in a hospital
for five years.
He was admitted as a teenager
and left a broken, wiser man.
He spent the years reading.
He memorized poetry.
He worked in the Springfield Armory
during WWII
because his broken body could not enlist.
His mind remembered the poetry.
His heart recited it to his children.
What he did for the war effort
was to build weapons for the soldiers.
What he did for all who fought and died
was to remember them.
Remember them
who were now at peace
Beneath the poppies row on row
beyond the war.
What he did was teach his children
the tender act
of remembering.

He taught his children
this day is not about freedom
or flag or beating our chests
for the freedom
to infect one another with
thoughtlessness.
This is a day to feel
the brokenness in our nation's bones,
to mourn lost souls,
to listen to voices of those who fought
on varied fronts and died
and remember who we are.
+

## Holding the Door

I saw a man
shuffle by
inside his jeans
too big
for him.

Unshaved chin
tucked into
a chest
concaved
somewhere
beneath
an old dress shirt.

Out of the
coffee shop,
he stopped
at the door
to hold it
open
for the person
walking with him.
But there was
No one there.

It was just
a muscle memory.

Even in a broken heart
love lingers in
a gesture
embedded
in our tissues.
+

## On the Edge of Tears

Living on the edge of tears.
The burning.
The welling.
The thickness around the throat.
The fear of the tears.
The blink back.
What good will it do?
Venting.
Purging.
A personal spillway
to prevent the dam from
breaking completely.
Perhaps.

A family vacation to
Niagara Falls took me to an edge.
A tunnel dug below the falls
to let the tourists stand in
ill-fitting raincoats and galoshes
reducing us all to children
giving us all the chance
to approach a wall of wet thunder,
to hear the roar, to feel the spray,
to touch the liquid rage if we dare.
I reached out. I felt the power of
it through my face.

I pulled back my hand lest it
grab me by the wrist
and kidnap me like a stranger
who feels nothing and
pounds on a riverbed
day and night.

Living on the edge of tears,
holding them back is not all bad.
In the space between reaching out
to the deluge and leaning away,
we discover a new muscle
and our own voice.
We want to live.
We want to hope.
Perhaps it is not always a bad thing
to hold back tears.
Perhaps it is our silent way of saying
I will choose the time for tears.
Not today. I will not add my tears today
to the overwhelming torrent.
I don't want to be someone else's
stranger grabbing them by the wrist.
Living on the edge of tears
can be an act of courage
and of hope. +

## An Extra Button

I can hear my mother's voice say,
"Do you have to say everything on your mind, Deb?"
I learned that my thoughts weren't welcome.
I feared none were welcome.
I started listening more than I spoke.
Not a bad thing.
Not a bad thing at all.
I learned to stop my thoughts from leaking out.
I have never been completely successful.
When the escapees got me in trouble,
I imagined needing a guardian at the gate.
I enlisted the back of my teeth
to cross their cuspids and crowns
like bayonets to prevent my words
from flying into the air
and detonating.

Now I wish for a more high-tech solution.
Before I hit the send button,
could someone invent a half-way house
or a holding tank
or a purgatory
where the words could sit
between good intentions and gut punch.
I would visit them again with questions.
Could they be received badly?

Could they be misunderstood?
Will they help at all?
What are my motives?
There is a satisfaction of hitting send,
but it is erased in the remorse
of unintended hurt or humblebrag.

An extra button would be nice
after the satisfying SEND.
A button appearing on the next screen
in a moment after the blood runs cooler
on the keyboard.
A button that asks, "Is this who you are?"

Until then, I am my own collector
of thoughts and my own guardian at the gate.
Until then, I take the risk to remain
silent and turn the weapons on myself
or take the risk to speak if only to say
"Take care. I hope this helps."
+

## Shekinah

One of the intimate horrors
of certain callings
is to tend to those
who have in that breath or hour
been told that
the one they loved
is dead.

The moment is so naked,
I have tended not
to stare but remain close.
I cannot touch their grief
I can only stand silently in it.

Once in a while,
I crossed my sight
into the sudden abyss of their shock,
plummeting into dark on dark,
colorless depths.
On one occasion I was surprised
by a veil of beauty.
A shekinah.
A light beyond human ability to radiate.
An aura the color of tenderness.

A brave whisper of hope amidst
the coming calendars of hurt

and hopelessness.

The agony of loss remains.
It does not heal before our eyes.
The wounds still bleed.
The infections still breed.
But sometimes, when least expected,
Shekinah shows her face
whose light holds all the colors for us
while we hurt.

The darkness of sorrow remains
and yet this morning
there is also an impossible
new shade of green
to be seen.

+

## The Room Where It Happens

Yes, I have the lyrics of the
musical Hamilton playing in a loop
and the loop threads into
my day, rise up
my projects, wait for it
mind at work, work, work
my news listening
to power brokers
and the wisdom seekers.
The one who asked to be
the last one in the room
before the decision was made.
The one invited to be
the last one in the room,
in the room where it happens.

If it were you
and the decision would impact
a life beyond your own,
who would you want for the last voice in your ear
before the door shut
and you were alone with the power
and the freedom to choose?

Now let us be honest.
there is no IF.

We are in the room where it happens.
Where the hate happens
and the greed and the grace,
and indifference.

The last voice in the room could be
the one most likely to agree with anything we say
the one most likely to disagree with anything we say
the one most likely to know what gives us joy, breaks our
hearts, or makes us mad
and holds up a mirror
before shutting the door
and leaving us in
the room where it happens.

We live with ourselves
everyday
in the room where it happens.
+

## Maundy Thursday 2020

Easter
is overrated.
Yeah, you heard me right.
This pandemic aftertaste
of drinking the lily-flavored Kool-Aid
of centuries of church histories,
theologies,
rituals.
Resurrection sermons fall flat
when we are talking about
something that hasn't happened
yet to anyone we know.
We wax it with metaphors
and music.
Dress up.
It still does not help Good Friday make any sense.

Now, Maundy Thursday,
is underrated.
Maundy means commandment
I know because I must look it up
every year because I forget.
The commandment is to love.
That's it.
Not rocket science.
Not resurrection.

Not miraculous healing.
Not dying.
The commandment is to love.
Feed the hungry.
Tend the sick.
Fight injustice.
That's what we need
right now.
Leave Easter to the lilies
and Jesus. They can be trusted with it.
The commandment is to love.
It is the only way through this
season of suffering.
The.
Only.
Way.
+

## Music as Second Language

I can read music,
but not well.
I can sing,
within a limited range.
I can appreciate
a song or a symphony
but not the accents
or nuances.

I know people for whom music
is their native language.
It is their sustenance,
bread and wine, divine,
drinkable, satiating,
rehydrating, detoxicating.
A pacemaker
returning hearts
to a lost rhythm.

I can hear the sound
but not understand
I am waiting
at a station without
a destination.
The trains of music rarely
stop at my heart.

Just now I needed the peace that
that had escaped me while
I waited for a storm to pass.
It made landfall further down the tracks
but my head could not calm down.
Music helps others,
why not me?

I heard the cacophony of my complaint.
I don't speak music!
I don't get it like others do.
Just then I heard
the thrum of my air conditioner.
The cicadas tuning.
The whirr of wheels on pavement,
life returning after evacuating.
The percussion of my dog panting in the shade
on this sunny day after a landfall just miles away,
just far enough away.

I drank the sounds in through my chest.
My heart was too thirsty to wait for me
and somehow it knew like an infant
how to drink the music in.

+

## ODE TO THE ELLIPSIS

Punctuation elegance.
Packed with mystery and joie de vivre.
Known more by its generic name,
dot dot dot
or conversationally,
yada yada yada.
You know what comes next.
It could also mean
none of us
know what comes next.
What if the Gospels had ended
with an ellipsis?
Or a death date on a tombstone?
Or tag, you're it.
I would bet you would choose the
dot dot dot.

Ellipsis is a writer's lazy go-to
when it is time to change the subject or
just find an ending. Somehow.
It could also be pregnant
with the next bold story or
just the old story we have heard
at least three dots worth of time ago.
I use it for all those purposes and more.
I use it when I want to break the grammar rules.

Being a rule-breaker
Means the colors are more important
Than the lines.
I use the ellipsis when I want you
To have a handhold to grasp like
a free climber on an impossibly steep ledge,
so that you can arrive at the summit
where the view is worth it...
I promise.
Or when we both know
that the ending is completely and utterly
in our hands...
Or not...
+

## Questions

If your life was a line, could it fly a kite?
What color is your pancreas?
If you were invisible, who could still see you?
What makes you cringe?
Who loves you?
What floats your boat?
What porks your chop?
How do hummingbirds fly in the rain?
How much money does it take to grow up?
What nickname makes you lean forward?
Is there an end to questions?
Can your curiosity be surgically removed?
Why do some people stop asking questions?
Why don't we take turns listening and being heard?
Why are we afraid of an answer we haven't heard yet?
What is your next great adventure?
What if your next great adventure is a person of a different flavor?
What if you are their next great adventure?
What is the question that you most want to answer?
What is the question that you most want to ask?
Is there fertilizer to grow love?

+

## The Endlings

You need to meet these two.
That is George.
Achatinella apexfulva. A species of snail.
That is Toughie.
A Rabb's fringe-limbed tree frog.
They were endlings.
Endlings are the last of their respective species.
When the species is down to its endling, it is
"functionally extinct."
Unable to breed because they are literally
All alone in the world.
They are no more.
George died early in 2019.
Toughie died in 2016.
A scientist, a human named David
cared for George for years.
A kind of hospice.
A sad duty to care for endlings.
It happens over and over again
and more frequently than ever
across the planet.
Mark, Toughie's caregiver,
heard Toughie vocalize two years ago
Singing for a mate.
There was no frog to hear his song.
Mark, a scientist, a human cried.

Humans need what humans need
and sometimes we don't pay attention
and worse, we don't care.

But there are scientists, humans like
David and Mark who spend their lives
sciencing...and caring.
I once shared the planet with George and Toughie.
Now I don't.
We could all be endlings one day.
But today, I share the planet
with other frogs and snails and
the Davids and Marks who care for them
and I like that.

*My thanks to Ed Yong, science writer for The Atlantic, without whose work, I wouldn't have known George, Toughie, David or Mark.*

+

## Rehab

Trust has never been a strong muscle of mine.
It got damaged early, often and severely
by the time I was tiptoe in my teens.
I do, however, flex survival.
I protected myself thoroughly and quickly.
It worked.
I survived.
It had side effects that would read as long as
the fine print of any pharmaceutical prescription.
The ones that are meant to make you give up
before it says, this stuff could kill you.

Survival without trust sucks breath.
An atrophied trust strangled
my own ability to survive.
How to trust myself to
make good decisions
recognize truth
be a vessel worthy of love,
an aqueduct for joy.
Fear did a good job keeping me alive.
I cannot fault it for doing that. I am grateful.
Trust in God did not come in a thunderstorm or a leap
of faith or an act of obedience.

I look back at my history now not as hobby

but signs of a life larger than my own.
I see the life-giving movement of the tender Spirit
nudging a dehydrated soul to water.
Repeatedly.
Patiently.
Relentlessly.
Hindsight gives me new lenses for the present.
I take baby steps with healing muscles of trust.
I am aware of others shuffling down this hallway
with the handrails.
None of us are whole.
We are all in rehab.
We have been nudged alive into this new day.
The muscles are stiff and uncertain.
It takes time
to learn to walk again.

+

## LANTANA

When I grow up,
I would like to be lantana for a season.
They sprawl.
No one would ever describe me that way,
but I would like the freedom to grow
wide and tall.
Unlike me, I would throw wild parties,
for bees, butterflies, birds humming in the band.
I would prank the neighbor by reaching
branches underneath the garage door as it closes
making it open again as they drove away.
Then I would grow where others couldn't reach
and push aside any attempt
at being tamed.

+

**I Wish**

I wish I knew what my dog thought about me.
I wish I could live as confidently as my bird.
I wish I could shut off the news. I can, but I can't.
I wish I would stop thinking
that I am a sum total of everything and everyone
I have encountered rather than believing
I am unique.

I wish Easter would happen more often.
I wish that a lot.
I don't want to hit "play again" on the Gospel story like
being caught in a groundhog movie
living the same day over and over again.
I wish we were not looking for a savior AGAIN.

I wish we were living our Easter life with passion,
compassion, justice, and joy.
I wish we were not standing on the road
looking for someone else to tell us what to do,
how to do the heavy lifting of love.
I wish we weren't so full of fear and ourselves.

I wish this year Easter was a call to arms
the kind of arms that stretch out
and love enormously and live
before they die and rise again.
I wish Easter was a way of life.

Is that too much to ask?
I wish the women who went to the tomb
heard laughter.
I wish they heard my dog talking about me
I wish the laughter they hear is
theirs and
mine
and yours.
+

About the Author

Deb Grant is a human living under the laws of gravity in Houston, Texas. Grant is the author of 6 previous books, Pedestrian Theology, ELOGOS Daily Devotions for Down to Earth Disciples 1,2, & 3, Passage, and STORM.

A native of New England, Grant earned her undergraduate degree from Barrington College (now Gordon College). She earned a Master of Divinity from Trinity Lutheran Seminary, Columbus, Ohio. Grant was ordained in 1981 serving as a pastor and campus pastor in the Evangelical Lutheran Church in America. After 37 years in ministry, Grant retired. She continues to write, create art pieces, care for her friends and help with charitable causes. Most of the time she is the humble servant to her dog and bird.

**Deb Grant's Contact Information:**
**Email**: revdeb@jazzwater.com
**Website:** www.jazzwater.com
**Etsy Shop:** www.etsy.com/shop/Jazzwater
**Facebook:** facebook.com/Elogosbydebgrant

**More copies of Nuevo Vino can be purchased at jazzwater.com.**

www.ingramcontent.com/pod-product-compliance
Lightning Source LLC
Chambersburg PA
CBHW051955290426
44110CB00015B/2258